White Magic Spell Book

Brittany Nightshade

Nightshade Apothecary Publishing

Copyright © 2020 Nightshade Apothecary LLC
All rights reserved. This book or any portion thereof may not be reproduced or used in any manner whatsoever without the express written permission of the publisher except for the use of brief quotations in a book review.

Table of Contents

Preface: 6
Spell Craft, Ritual Work, and Intention 8
Calling Quarters and Elements 14
    Creating a Circle 16
    Elemental Circle Casting Ritual 19
White Magic 21
    Moon Water 22
    Moon Phases 24
    Sea Water 26
    Sage Cleansing (Smudging) 28
    Invocation of Hecate 30
    Invocation of Nyx, Goddess of Night 35
    Bonding with a Familiar 38
    Black Salt 40
    Jar Spells 41
    Protection Jar 43
    Home Protection Crystal Enchantment 45
    Confidence Tea Ritual 47
    Ancestral Communion 48

- To Find Closure 50
- Clairvoyance Spell 52
- To Bless a Relationship........................ 53
- Rune of Protection 55
- Protection Potion................................ 56
- Protection from Storms 57
- Calming Spell 59
- Spell of Protection 60
- Old and Grey.. 61
- Financial Prosperity............................. 62
- Remove Evil from an Object................. 63
- Healing a Broken Heart 65
- Witch Bottle (Curse Removal/Protection) 66
- Chant to Bring Rain 68
- Banishing Spell..................................... 70
- Banishment Sigil................................... 71
- Protection Stone 73
- Goal Accomplishment Jar Spell 74
- Aphrodite Beauty Oil............................ 77
- To Prevent Nightmares 79

- Basic Healing Spell 80
- Pentacle Ward Spell 81
- Cleansing/Charging a New Wand 82
- Garden Growth Spell............................ 84
- Second Sight, Third Eye Ritual 86
- Ritual of Undoing 88
- Sigil Magic... 90
- Divination 97
  - Rune Casting 100
  - Three Norns Method.......................... 100
  - Scrying 102
  - Pendulum Dowsing 103
- The Futhark Runes 106
- In Closing 157

Preface:

Merry Meet!

My name is Brittany Nightshade and I've spent many years studying witchcraft and Pagan tradition. While on my journey I've did my best to keep a record of the rituals and anything magical I've learned along the way. I've taken some of the White Magic Rituals I've collected in my book of shadows to make this spell book of white magic.

This book has a wide assortment of White Magic spells and rituals for beginners and advanced spell-casters. There's also a section on divination with a guide to the Futhark Runes, these runes are great for divination and can be incorporated into your own spells and rituals. I've also included dowsing charts and a wheel calendar in the back of the book for reference.

Whether you use these spells to craft your own rituals or use them as they are, remember the power is inside of you. There is no requirement to use exact recipes and from my experience when you personalize a spell it only makes it stronger as it's all about being able to focus your intentions. If a ritual in this book calls for a certain god or goddess and you don't feel a connection with that god you are free to change it to anything that helps you conduct your ritual more effectively. Only through meditation and practice will your powers grow so don't be afraid of making mistakes or not having the perfect ritual, it's all about you and your energies! I wish you the best of luck in your magical endeavors. <3

Spell Craft, Ritual Work, and Intention

The first thing that comes to many people's minds when they hear the word 'witch' is magic. Unfortunately, most people have been misinformed of what magic is as it pertains to witchcraft.

The common misconceptions that have plagued history insinuate that witches have the ability to transmute humans into animals, shapeshift, control fire and lightning with their minds, disappear and reappear at will, levitate, and every other Hollywood trope you can imagine. While this might have been entertaining and at times stoked fears that go back thousands of years, the reality is much more down to earth, pun intended, and pragmatic in nature.

A witch's magic is more akin to what most would call 'prayer.' It might come as a shock that many witches also refer to their ritual work as prayer. After all, what is a prayer but a ritual done with the aim of working with a deity or the cosmos to achieve a desired outcome?

Witches use magic to accomplish a number of things. Magic can protect, bewitch, influence, boost confidence, and imbue energies into charms, talismans and other mundane objects. It can alter the threads of fate and be used to honor and revere our gods, goddesses, ancestors, and the many other facets of nature.

It should be said that rituals and spells aren't necessarily the same thing. Spells usually involve some sort of ritual, but rituals don't always involve spell work/magic. Magic spells are done to achieve an outcome, such as healing from heartbreak or binding an abusive person. We achieve these outcomes through meditation and the direction of our intentions to affect the world around us. To aid in the proper direction and channeling of our intention and energies we generally employ ritual work.

However, ritual work doesn't always have to involve trying to receive or affect something. We also use rituals to honor and commune with our deities or with nature itself, depending on your chosen path. This is integral to most witches as they bond with their gods and goddesses and grow in power through their faith and dedication.

A witch's spell might be said over a boiling cauldron like you see in the movies, but it is more likely that witchcraft involves a ceremony that can be performed in nature, on the witch's home altar, in their kitchen, or in a coven setting. The place that works best for you is the one that allows you to achieve maximum concentration and connection with the spirit world.

Spells might be cast to affect the castor, other people, or to influence energies to cause some sort of change and can be beneficial or harmful. Spells that are positive in nature are often called blessings, while negative spells are generally called hexes or curses. Spells can also be used to prevent something from happening. These are called binding spells and can be positive or negative in nature depending on the intent.

The classification of certain magics as white, black, positive, negative, grey, etc., is hotly debated in the wider Wiccan community. Many argue that the intent of the practitioner is what gives a spell or ritual its designation, while many others argue that magic is magic and we're not meant to try to put ritual work into boxes. Most traditional Wiccans take a no-nuance approach to any magic that affects or influences the will of another and considers them a violation of the Wiccan rede. On the other hand, many Eclectic Witches believe you must look at each situation on a case-by-case basis to determine whether the spell is justified. You may have your own way of determining this and morality is subjective. I choose to consult with The Norns, the Norse Goddesses of Fate, before I set out to make any changes in the world with my ritual work and I regularly consult with Hecate on day-to-day matters and self-development, I do this through meditative prayer and divination.

A ritual typically has a formula that the practitioner has crafted or received from another witch or their coven. It's quite common, and many have argued beneficial, to adapt a ritual to fit your needs. Spells can involve incantations, imagery, runes, candles, and other magical tools. Offerings are commonly made to the practitioner's god or goddess as part of a ritual ceremony of reverence.

There are many methods to cast spells. You might inscribe runes or sigils onto an object, like a ring or a necklace, to imbue it with certain properties. You could burn the picture of a romantic interest as part of the ritual for a love spell. You can even brew up a potion to use in your bath to make yourself more charismatic. There are virtually countless ways to go about crafting a spell. The most important part is that you feel a connection with what you're doing because that's the secret to successful spell crafting. Uncertainty and doubt are usually the cause of a spells failure, confidence is key, know that the details aren't as important as you directing your energies where they need to go through visualization and manifestation.

Ritual work and spell casting doesn't have to be complicated. A ritual can be as simple as lighting a candle or incense while thinking about the safety and protection of your family. For day-to-day spells, such as blessings, self-help, positive thoughts and the sending of helpful healing energies to others, it is not necessary to undertake the cumbersome task of a full circle-casting ritual. Although these intricacies can be useful for beginners in helping with concentration and immersion. To honor your ancestors, you could simply set them a place at the table with offerings of food and wine. Before bed, you can speak to your goddess and give her thanks for all the blessings she bestows upon your life. Just do what makes you feel good and what you think is the best way to worship and establish a connection to the magical world.

Calling Quarters and Elements

In witchcraft the Quarters refer to the elements of nature. These elements are forces that are revered by many pagans. They might be called by another name, but you will commonly hear them referred to as elements, elementals, watchtowers, corners, or quarters. These different terms might have slightly different meanings depending on the practitioner, but they all have a similar role in witchcraft.

The pentacle represents the four elements. The divine, or the practitioner, is the top point of the pentacle with the four elements making up the side points. This represents how the practitioner, or the divine within the practitioner, guides and acts as a conduit for the elemental forces. This is the most common interpretation, although views might differ from witch to witch, but as a general rule most witches incorporate the elements into their rituals in one way or another.

The four corners refer to the cardinal points of the compass: north, south, east and west. They might also refer to the four classical elements: water, earth, fire, and air. A fifth element that is often included in some Eastern traditions is 'The Void', or that which we can't see. Most western traditions consider the self, or the spirit, to be the fifth.

Many techniques are derived from different traditions and a witch may try different things or adapt and create their own rituals until they find something that works for them. The tradition of witchcraft spans across many different cultures and is a constantly evolving, living belief which is why you will find such variation in practice.

Many witches make use of the elements, seeing them as inter-connected energies that make up everything we see and experience. Practitioners will often call the Guardians of the Watchtowers to keep the energies stable and unaffected while channeling. As you develop your powers you'll likely have your own unique way of channeling the elements. In the next section I'll go over different methods that you could use and adapt to cast your own circle.

Creating a Circle

Witches may create a circle to prepare a magical, sacred space to meditate, cast a spell or perform a ritual. The circles are actually spheres that are used as a type of insulation from unwanted energies which might affect the spell, ritual, or meditation. This helps prevent the misdirection of intention during spell work or the interruption of energy transference. Circles aren't necessary, but in my opinion, can greatly aid in concentration.

A circle can be cast by simply holding out your finger, wand, athame or staff and turning 360 degrees in a clockwise motion. The circle can be closed after you are done by doing the same but in reverse (counterclockwise) or by cutting the boundary of the circle with your athame, wand, or hand. This is an easy and effective way to cast a circle, but you might also wish to incorporate an invocation or ritual of your own design. It doesn't matter how you cast your circle; the key is having faith in what you are doing so you can effectively use your energy to create the barrier.

A popular method of casting a circle involves incorporating the elements and cardinal directions into the casting. For example, you might want to place an object representing each element in each direction you will be pointing to while casting the circle or call upon the guardians and elements themselves. The following are examples of what might be used to represent each element, but you may use anything that you personally associate with the element.

Air/East: sword, athame, wand, feathers, bells, ribbons, Ace of Swords Tarot.

Fire/South: candles, thorns, wands and other phallic objects, dragons, matches, masculine aspect, Ace of Wands Tarot.

Water/West: chalice, cup, seashells, crystal ball, ankh, mirror, water/wine, feminine aspect, Ace of Cups Tarot.

Earth/North: pentacle, altar, metals, coins, flowers/herbs, soil, sand, salt, nuts and seeds, Ace of Pentacles Tarot.

Elemental Circle Casting Ritual

With your wand or other tool in your dominant hand point towards the east side of the circle and say the following:

"I call upon the Guardian of the East, Element of Air, to watch over this sacred space."

Envision the Guardian appearing in the east, bow to acknowledge the Guardian, and turn to the south. With your hand extended say the following:

"I call upon the Guardian of the South, Element of Fire, to watch over this sacred space."

Envision the Guardian, bow to acknowledge him, and turn to the west. With your hand extended say the following:

"I call upon the Guardian of the West, Element of Water, to watch over this sacred space."

As you envision the arrival of the Guardian, bow in respect, and turn to the north. With your arm still extended, say the following:

"I call upon the Guardian of the North, Element of Earth, to watch over this sacred space."

Raise your hand up into the air and say the following:

"I call upon the spirit to protect this space, as I will, the circle is cast."

White Magic

Magic doesn't necessarily have an official color system, but people usually will describe it as white or light if the spell doesn't harm or influence the will of another. White Magic is the safest of all spell types and is a good place to start if you're a beginner because there's no potentially negative consequences to misdirecting your intention.

Healing and protection rituals are some of the oldest spells known. Healers were integral parts of pagan villages and their studies in herbalism and health are what went on to become modern medicine. These spells are an important part of any witch's arsenal and will prepare you for anything you encounter on your path.

Moon Water

Moon water is used in spells, potions, cleansing and charging sigils: pretty much any witchcraft practice where you use water and need the power and protection of the moon. This water can also be placed on your altar and used as a representation of the Element of Water and the moon. The only essential part of a ritual to make moon water is the presence of the moon in the night sky. You can simply place your jar in a windowsill or do a complex ritual invoking a deity.

You will need:
One clear glass jar or bottle with lid
Water
A place to safely place your jar outside at night

Fill your container with water and place it outside or in a window once the moon has risen in the sky. You may say a prayer to any gods or goddesses of your choosing if you so wish - this is especially helpful if you plan on using your water in a ritual involving said deities. Common Lunar Goddesses you might want to call to are Selene, Artemis, Hecate, Diana, Bastet, Luna, Astarte, or Phoebe.

Example Moon Water Blessing Ritual calling upon Hecate:

Say the following in the presence of the moon once the sun is completely out of sight.

"I call upon the Grace of Hecate,
I ask of you to grant your blessings and power to me on this night of most importance.
Fill me and my Lunar Water with your divine grace so that I may fulfill my purposes and bring blinding clarity into the darkness as you have always done."

Place your jar out for an hour or so or retrieve it in the morning, don't worry about the jar coming into contact with sunlight as your intention was to charge the jar with moonlight and the suns light can't simply undo that.

Moon Phases

Moon water can be charged under any phase of the moon and different phases can be used for different types of moon water, although it's not necessary. These phases and their strengths can be applied to your other spell work as well.

Full moon: healing, charging, banishing, love magic, cleansing, protection

Waning gibbous: cleansing, relinquishing, undoing curses and bindings

Last quarter: breaking curses and bad habits, banishing, relinquishing

Waning crescent: success, curing illness, attaining wisdom, balance, atonement

Dark moon: soul searching, banishing, divination, deconstruction, binding

Waxing crescent: wealth, luck, constructive magic, friendship, attraction, success

First quarter: motivation, divination, calming, strength, growth

Waxing gibbous: success, good health, attraction, motivation

New moon: new relationships, love, new beginnings, change, liminal spaces

Sea Water

Sea/ocean water can be used by a witch for a myriad of things. It's great for cleansing and can be used in a spray bottle or as a bath for any magic or mundane objects. You can also set a jar or bottle of it on your altar to represent both Water and Earth elements.

It's not always easy to collect your own sea water, but fortunately you can make some yourself that's just as effective. You can work with any god/goddess with dominion over the sea. In this ritual, I'll be working with Amphitrite, the wife of Poseidon, but you can also work with Hecate who is also honored and worshiped as a sea goddess.

What you will need:
Hot water (2 cups)
Seashell
Sea salt (4 pinches)
Container for mixing

Mix your sea salt and water until all the salt is dissolved. Hold your seashell in your hand and loudly say the following:

*"Amphitrite! Queen of the Sea!
I ask that you lend your power to this vessel!
Mighty goddess of the deep!
I welcome you and give you thanks!"*

Drop your shell into the water and the ritual is complete.

Remember to give thanks to your god or goddess when using your sea water.

Sage Cleansing (Smudging)

You can cleanse anything with the smoke from sage. This is either done with a sage stick (smudge stick) or by burning sage in an incense burner. Sage has powerful cleansing properties and can be used to cleanse your home, altar space, jewelry, crystals, candles or any other ritual tool or object. Sage can also be used to cleanse yourself. Other common incense used for cleansing are myrrh and dragons blood, but I typically use sage. (Make sure that your sage is ethically sourced, many big box chain stores get their sage for unsustainable sources that harm the areas in which they're harvested. This is especially important if you're using white sage. I highly suggest growing your own, it's easy and will strengthen your connection nature.

To cleanse your home set your intention to cleanse, light your sage and allow it to burn out and smolder. Carry the sage throughout the house and allow the smoke to flow into the rooms. Pay special attention to mirrors, hallways, and other high traffic areas. As you do this you can say a prayer to a goddess or an incantation to better focus your intention.

To cleanse an object, do the same thing: set your intention, light your sage and run the object through the smoke. If the object is large, take the sage and move it around the object, letting the smoke envelope it.

To cleanse yourself, light your sage and allow it to burn out, take the smoke with your hands and direct it around your body. "Wash" your hands, face, body, legs, etc. with the smoke. Do this with the intent of cleansing and purification.

Invocation of Hecate
Devotion and Dedication Ritual

Hecate is the mother of all witches and the Greek goddess of witchcraft, magic, and the sea. She holds the keys to the underworld and can equally protect from the spirits of the underworld or send them to attack. She's known as a liminal goddess, meaning she freely crosses between realms of Earth, Heaven and Hades, and can walk through the veil that separates the three. Hecate is known as the Triple Moon Goddess and holds dominion over the Earth, Heavens and Sea, and wields immeasurable power as a daughter of Titans and the matron goddess of witches.

If you acquire her favor, she will shield you from the unjust and bring you creativity, wisdom, and guidance. She is darkness. She is everything. As you develop a relationship with her you will find that the knowledge and wisdom needed to bring forth light resides in the mysteries and blessings of the dark.

It helps if you are in a meditative state when calling out to her, but you do not have to be. I find my connection to her to be strongest at night. Since she represents all phases of the moon it doesn't have to be at a certain time of month, but the new moon is ideal. It would help if you incorporate one or more of her symbols. For instance, some of Hecate's symbols are the moon, keys, black, silver, darkness, crossroads, the number three, and dogs. There are many more and you should learn about each individually and why they represent her as that will strengthen your connection and understanding of her. Place these items on your altar or hold them during the invocation.

Focus on the symbol and what it represents, open up your mind and be willing to accept her energies. If possible, light a black candle. Place offerings such as wine, food or incense on your altar or ritual space. Common offerings to Hecate are honey, fish, garlic, eggs, and wine. You should always make offerings to show your thanks and dedication when you work with Hecate. Offerings can simply be placed upon your altar or workspace and you can do with them what you wish after the ritual is concluded although some people like to leave wine on their altars until some of the liquid has evaporated.

The following prayer is an invocation I've created to call upon Hecate and devote oneself to her path. You can use my ritual or develop your own devotional ritual just as you can for any of the invocations in this book.

Clear your thoughts and let the image fill your mind, then begin to relax. Concentrate on your energy connecting with the darkness, feel your energies being aligned with hers and say the following:

"Hecate, Mother of Darkness, I call upon you!

I am answering your call and am ready to dedicate myself to your path!
Goddess of Night, protect me with your arcane power!
Grant me the sight to see through the veil and attain the wisdom you grant!
Maiden of thresholds and crossroads surround me in your darkness so that I can bring forth my light!
Dark Mother! I pledge my loyalty!
I honor you now and forever! By the power of the Triple Moon!

Hail Hecate! Hail Hecate! Hail Hecate! "

As your relationship with Hecate develops, you'll find your own way of worshiping and communicating with her. Each relationship is different and deeply personal. She can be demanding but will never fault or punish you for your shortcomings so never hesitate to seek her out and let her torch guide you through any turmoil you may face.

Pray to Hecate regularly. I normally hold a ritual on the new moon and give thanks and offerings daily. Cherish the bond you have with her as her grace will be a blessing that will protect and lead you through the void.

Invocation of Nyx, Goddess of Night

Nyx is the primordial Goddess of Night. She is a daughter of Chaos and has been here since the beginning of time itself. It is said that even the mighty Zeus feared her. This ritual is meant to create a bond with this ancient goddess of unfathomable power.

You will need:
Blessing oil
Altar
Full moon drawn on an altar cover
Sage
Sweet grass
Red rose petals
Black rose petals
1 red candle
1 blue candle
1 purple candle
1 black candle
1 white candle

Smudge the altar, the candles, and yourself with the sage. Place the sage on the altar (use a fireproof vessel or plate for the sage). Place the five candles on the altar with black in the north, white in the east, red in the south, and blue in the west with purple in the middle. Light them in this order: black, white, red, blue, purple.

Say the following:

"Nyx, great Goddess of the Night! Lover of Erebus, mother of Moros, Thanatos, Hypnos, Charon, Nemesis, and the Fates, I ask you to accept my loyalty and my love as your follower and servant. I ask for your protection and guidance, bringer of the night, I ask for your wisdom and blessings."

Re-light the sage if it burnt out and light up the sweet grass (if you don't have sweet grass you can use any other type of incense). Use the sweet grass to smudge the altar, the candles, the rose petals, and yourself. Place the sweet grass next to the sage and let it burn out as you visualize Nyx sending you her protection, wisdom, guidance, and blessing. Once the sweet grass and the sage burn out sprinkle the petals into the gaps between the candles and the herbs from your hands as you chant:

"I am [your name]. I am a Priest/Priestess for my Goddess, you, Nyx, if you will have me.
This is my request, and these are my words.
May this oath stay strong, my faith never wavers, my love never weakens.
Blessings of Nyx, wash over me!"

Honor Nyx with offerings and prayer and she will always answer your call. There are many gods and goddesses, I suggest learning about as many as you can and find the ones that resonate with your personal energies. Spend time learning about them and make your own rituals using inspiration from the invocations in this book or craft your own from scratch! I would imagine any god or goddess would be impressed with someone who took the time to craft their own ritual for them, don't worry about the details, it's literally the thought that counts.

Bonding with a Familiar

A familiar is an animal or nature spirit that you can bond with that can assist you in your practice. Familiars can lend you their energies and protect against malevolent forces. Some bonds happen naturally but you can also perform a ritual to attempt to create a familiar bond.

Embrace the animal or envision the spirit you wish to bond with and say the following:

"A bond to be made in (god, goddess, or entities) name,
I ask for your assistance,
Keep me safe from all that'd harm,
And counter all resistance.
Together we can do great things,
No matter what the 'morrow brings."

Meditate on the connection between your spirit and theirs: you will feel the connection when it's made. If the spell didn't work keep in mind that not every spirit wants to or is ready to be your familiar and you stand a much greater chance if you have already built a connection with spirit you are trying to enlist. As you grow in experience you might find that familiars will call to you and your ability to bond with them will grow.

Black Salt

Black salt is an ingredient that is commonly used in witchcraft and can be made from simple household items. Black salt is a powerful protective ingredient and tool that can be used as part of any greater ritual that calls for any kind of salt or simply spread around the home or kept in a sachet for protection.

You will need:
Sea salt
Ashes

The simplest way to make black salt is to take some ashes from your incense burner or fireplace and grind 2 parts salt with 1 parts ash. As you mix the ingredients, be sure to charge the salt with protective intent.

You may also add other protective ingredients such as eggshells, cinnamon, or a pinch of ethically acquired graveyard dirt. When acquiring graveyard dirt be sure to leave an offering such as tobacco, salt or sugar.

Jar Spells

Jar spells are an old form of folk magic that can be done in a variety of ways for a near limitless number of purposes. The maker sets/defines their intent and places charged objects into a jar. The jar is then sealed and ceremoniously discarded. Protection jars are typically buried or hidden away although some spells call for the destruction of the jar. The specifics of the jars aren't important: the intent and your focus are what makes everything work.

The first step is to define and set your intentions, know exactly what you want and keep focused. You can also write your intention on a piece of paper to be placed in the jar during the ritual. You then fill your jar with objects related to your intent, such as crystals, spices, herbs, liquids and anything else you wish to use.

Place the items in one by one, charge each item by focusing your intent into them as you place them into the jar. After everything is in the jar, you must seal it so the energies within the bottle are contained. You can do this by dripping candle wax on the seal or letting the candle burn down onto the jar. If your lid is plastic, you'll need to place fireproof paper between the candle and lid. You can also use string, glue, honey, or anything else that would work to keep the jar energetically sealed.

The jar can now be buried, destroyed or hidden away so they may work their magic. You can also make small jars and carry them with you. I keep a small protection jar with me whenever I leave the house.

Protection Jar

This jar will work to protect the maker or anyone they focus their intentions on while crafting it. Change up the ingredients to fit your own style if you'd like. I use ingredients that are generally known for their protective qualities.

You will need:
Jar
White candle
Dirt or sand
Crystal (quartz or black tourmaline)
White pepper
Basil leaf
Cinnamon (powder or stick)
Shell

Cleanse your ingredients and place them on your altar or ritual space with your jar.

Meditate on your intent for a moment, for example, the need to be safe and protected from harm. If you're seeking protection from a specific thing, concentrate on that thing and its inability to hurt you.

Maintain your focus as you pour the dirt or sand into your jar. This is your base. Continue to place each item in one at a time all while directing your energies and intent into the items.

Light the white candle and allow the wax to drip on the seal of the jar. You may also place the candle on top of the jar and let it completely burn down, coating the jar in wax.

The jar can now be hidden away or buried. The jar could be placed behind a wall, in the back of a closet, under your bed or even built into the walls of your house. If your jar is small enough you can even carry it with you.

Home Protection Crystal Enchantment

You will need:
Large crystal
Large bowl or cauldron
Water
Sea salt
Basil
Something from your home/yard
Wand or something to stir the water

Place your crystal in the cauldron and fill it with enough water to cover the crystal. Throw a pinch of salt into the cauldron and say the following:

"Bless this family and bless this home,
While we're here and while we roam,
When darkness beckons our light will shine,
And protect the ones that I call mine."

Throw in a pinch of basil and something from your yard or home. It can be a rock, a leaf, a blade a grass or even a fiber from your carpet. It just needs to be something that has a connection to the property you are blessing.

Use your wand to stir the water in a clockwise motion. Do 7 complete circles around the crystal while stirring.

Display the crystal in a common area of the home.

Confidence Tea Ritual

This is a simple morning tea ritual to get your positive energy flowing and to set our intentions for the day.

You will need:
Your favorite type of tea
Your favorite teacup

Brew the tea and and pour into your favorite cup while saying the following:

*"Confident, beautiful, secure and grand,
I hold the future in the palm of my hand,
I'll conquer the day and reap the rewards,
While always moving forever forwards."*

Relax and drink your tea while thinking of all the things you're going to accomplish today.

Ancestral Communion

The reverence of our ancestors is a common part of many pagan practices, we honor our ancestors and reach out to them for guidance. Use this ritual to open up a spiritual link between you and your ancestors.

You will need:
Athame (ritual dagger)
White candle
Ansuz rune
Offerings

Inscribe the rune onto the candle with your athame. Light the candle and sit in a comfortable position. Place your offerings in front of you or on your altar. Meditate on the Futhark rune, Ansuz, which is used in Ancestral Magic. Allow the rune to open up a connection to the person you are trying to connect with.

For as long as you see fit, meditate on the person you are trying to contact. Pay homage to this person's life and reminisce on any memories you have of them.
Say the following incantation:

"I feel the warmth of your body and soul.
I welcome you here, my heart is whole.
Please come to me, (optional: insert name)."

If the person has answered your call, you will feel their presence. You may get a chill or even feel warmth depending on the circumstances.

You will likely just feel their energy, but if you are experienced enough it's possible to hear or even see them. It's also quite common after an invitation is made for them to visit you in your dreams where communication is much easier. If the spell isn't successful, try it once again before going to sleep.

Use this ritual to honor your ancestors. Consider setting a place at your dining table with the offerings as part of the ritual. Enjoy their presence and give thanks for their protections and blessings. Speak with them and listen to what they have to say. After you've made contact and accomplished what you set out to do make sure to thank them for coming and tell them that you both must be on your way.

To Find Closure

This ritual is meant to help you find closure after a relationship has come to an end. This can be a romantic relationship or a friendship that has gone sour. Sometimes our past weighs heavy on our minds and this ritual can be a great way to put your first foot forward down a new path with new opportunities.

You will need:
Red candle
Blue candle
Black candle
Incense

Light the candles and the incense and say the following:

*"As you leave my life,
I leave behind my pain.
As you scatter like dust,
So does all my hurt.
As I leave you in my past,
I leave with you my sorrow."*

Take a moment to reflect on how much you've learned and grown since before the relationship. Imagine how you'll use this knowledge going forward and starting a new chapter in your life, better prepared and wiser than you ever were before.

Clairvoyance Spell

This spell will allow you to see people's true intentions and will give you the power to see through any illusion or manipulation.

You will need:
Amber incense
Blue candle

Light the candle and the incense and say the following:

"Veritas, Goddess of Truth!
Grant me the power to see through the lies,
To see the intention in everyone's eyes,
Deception be damned, illusions be gone
A sight that can be counted on"

Make sure to give thanks to Veritas for your new fledgling gift of clairvoyance, work on this skill through meditation, this ritual can be repeated whenever you want as a ritual to Veritas. As your connection with Veritas grows your powers of clairvoyance will as well.

To Bless a Relationship

A simple ritual to do with your significant other to ensure a long-lasting and happy relationship.

You will need:
Loaf of bread
Wine glass
Othala rune

Bake a fresh loaf of bread. Hold it up to the moon and ask the gods and goddesses to bless the bread as well as the relationship. Break off a piece of the bread for your partner, as well as one for yourself, and fill the glass you'll be sharing with a beverage of your choice.

Incorporate the Othala rune in any way you'd like. You can etch or draw it onto the wine glass, bake it into the bread design or simply draw it on a piece of paper and use it as a coaster for the glass.

As you share time together, share the bread as well. Do not cut the bread with a knife or any other cutting tool. Just break off the pieces with your hands. The bread may be any type you like and you can add butter, jam, or anything else that you and your partner might like.

Rune of Protection

"Algiz, Rune of Life"

Algiz is a powerful rune of protection and can either be drawn on paper and placed or etched somewhere close, like on your altar, clothing, ritual tools, or your body. It can also be used in crafting your own protection spells. Algiz is one of the most common runes found amongst archeological finds in Scandinavia and was commonly placed on the shields of warriors before going into battle.

Protection Potion

This potion acts as a ward to any spirits with ill-intentions. Vervain has been used for centuries as a ward against vampires and works against any malicious spirit. Basil has also been used for protection against the evil eye, which is where someone is essentially casting negative energies at you with their gaze.

You will need:
1/2 cup of water
1 teaspoon vervain or 5 drops of vervain Oil
2 tablespoons sea salt
1 teaspoon of basil or 5 drops of basil oil
Glass jar

Lightly sprinkle the potion around your home in discreet places (i.e. in closets) and anoint the bottom of your shoes and those of your loved ones. This potion can also be used as a powerful ritual ingredient for any spells pertaining to protection.

Protection from Storms

This spell works to grant you and your loved ones safety from inclement weather. Thurisaz is a rune that represents loss, pain and hardship, we'll be reversing that rune to and using it in a ritual to ask that we be spared from those hardships.

"Thurisaz reversed"

With your dominant hand, write the reversed Thurisaz Rune in the air in the direction of the storm.

Say the following:

*"Children of the winds, Guardians of Air, Listen to my words. Harken to my prayer.
Breathe upon me gently.
Breathe upon me warm.
Guard my home and family.
Keep us safe from harm.
In Thor's name,
So Mote it Be!"*

Calming Spell

This is a simple spell to bring about calmness in oneself. Once this spell is mastered, it can even be used to calm those around you.

Look deeply at the palm of your hand and chant the following until you can feel the calm overtaking you, if you're in a public setting you can also chant the mantra in your mind:

*"As I look into my palm,
The goddess grants the gift of calm."*

As you repeat the mantra study the lines of your hands, see how the creases intersect, interconnected as all things are. Repeat until peace rushes over your body.

Spell of Protection

A basic protection spell that will help you focus and prevent the misdirection of your intentions. This spell is also useful for creating a barrier against the ill-will of others.

Draw a pentacle in front of you and say the following:

"By the power of the five-point star,
spirits be you near or far,
I call on thee, hear this cry,
spirits that protect come now and fly,
spirits now I ask of thee,
protect me from dark energy,
so mote it be... so mote it be... so mote it be."

Old and Grey

This is a ritual to ensure that you and the one you love will outlast all the challenges life may throw at you. All obstacles can be overcome with a strong will and a bit of magic!

You will need:
Hair from you and your loved one
Small rose quartz
Small pouch

Place the hair and the rose quartz crystal into the pouch and say the following:

> *"Until the sun no longer shines,*
> *Long life and health to me and mine,*
> *The storms we'll weather,*
> *the mountains we'll climb,*
> *Our love will remain,*
> *until the end of time."*

Hold the pouch and meditate on the wonderful future you and your beloved will have. Keep the pouch in a safe place.

Financial Prosperity

This is a wealth spell that is designed to give you the strength and confidence you need to achieve success, while also asking the gods to send opportunities and show you the path to achieve your goals.

You will need:
Sage or jasmine incense
Yellow and green candle
Something representing your god/goddess

Light the candles on your altar on either side of your representation and say the following:

"Day by day, I waste away,
No time to wait, I can't delay,
Grant me the strength, to rise above,
Send opportunity and wealth my way."

Close your eyes, envision your future successes and meditate on how you'll go about achieving your goals. When you're ready to end the ritual, thank your god/goddess and blow out the candles.

Remove Evil from an Object

This ritual can be used to remove evil or cursed/negative energies or entities from any object.

You will need:
1 white candle
Salt
Cursed object
Pentacle
Black cloth
Tourmaline crystal

Set the object down on the black cloth and put the pentacle on top of it, if you can't put it on top of the object just make sure that it's touching it. Light the candle and put it in front of the object.

Take your salt and use it to draw a circle around your object, making sure the circle is as thick and perfect as you can make it, I like to make my salt circles about ½ an inch in thickness but as long as the circle is complete it will work.

Place the tourmaline so that's it bordering the circle of salt on the outside, during the ritual you'll be breaking the salt circle to open up a path to the crystal.

Say the following:

> *"Positive energy, stay with me,*
> *Negative energy leave me be.*
> *Leave, you don't belong here,*
> *Go far away, never near.*
> *I demand all evil to flee.*
> *I demand that you listen to me.*
> *Get out, get out, get out.*
> *Leave, leave. Hear my shout.*
> *This is my will so mote it be."*

Now clear out a path through the salt that leads to your tourmaline crystal, the cursed energies contained within the object will exit the circle and be neutralized by the tourmaline as it tries to escape.

Healing a Broken Heart

This is a ritual for healing a broken heart, ending a dying relationship, and starting anew. Do this spell under a full or new moon.

Call upon your goddess/god of choice and say the following chant until you feel the pain lift from your heart:

> *"Oh Goddess, take my pain,*
> *Steady as a falling rain.*
> *Give me courage to call an end,*
> *Give me a chance to start again.*
> *Help heal all the broken hearts,*
> *So that we may easily part.*
> *Oh, Goddess let my will be done,*
> *With no harm to anyone.*
> *Blessed Be! So mote it be!"*

Visualize yourself in your mind, happy, and ending with ease and starting new and fresh. See new beginnings and happy times with no more pain ahead for yourself.

Witch Bottle (Curse Removal/Protection)

Witch bottles have been used in folk magic for hundreds of years to break curses and protect the maker from another witch's magical attack. They are a type of jar spell.

You will need:
Jar or bottle
Salt
Black candle
Something from the victim
Bent nails or pins
Urine or wine

Do this like any other jar spell. Focus your intention. In this instance, it's the removal of a curse or protection from magical attack. Place each object in one at a time. Start with the salt for your base followed by the item from you or the people you're trying to protect. This can be fingernails, hair, teeth, a picture or anything connected to them. Place your nails and/or pins in next, followed by the urine or wine.

Close the jar and seal it with the black candle wax. Bury the jar in your yard, concluding the ritual. This jar serves as a sort of decoy for any negative energies, trapping them beneath the earth and leaving you free from harm.

Chant to Bring Rain

This spell will utilize the Berkano rune to encourage growth in the surrounding flora. To be able to grow and flourish the surrounding plants will need water. Once you set these energies into motion it won't be long until rain finds its way to you to fulfill this need.

(Berkano, Rune of Growth)

Draw the Berkano rune in the ground outside and say the following:

*"Goddess bring the rain down,
Giving life unto the ground.
Energy to feed the seed,
Mother-natures gift to me.*

Goddess bring the rain down,
Giving life unto the ground.
Energy to feed the seed,
And a healthy harvest bring.
As in my will, so mote it be!"

Banishing Spell
(Spirit and Demon Banishment)

If you find you are being haunted by a spirit, demon, or other supernatural entity you will need to cast a banishing spell to rid yourself of their presence.

What you will need:
Enough salt to draw a pentacle.
Citrine crystal or selenite
A room with a window

Draw a pentacle on the ground or on your altar with the salt, place your crystal in the middle of the pentacle, open your window and chant the following three times:

*"Ashes to ashes, dust to dust,
Return from whence you came,
You are no longer welcome, it's time to go,
I do this in Hecate's name!"*

Close your window and remove the pentacle to complete the spell.

Banishment Sigil

If the previous spell didn't work and you can't seem to rid yourself of your unwanted spirits, you could try this sigil.

Dr. Johannes Faust wrote a book called *The Black Raven* on the summoning and binding of spirits in the early 1500s. In the pages of this manic document are many sigils that serve different purposes when summoning spirits. One of these sigils claims to have the power to banish evil spirits.

I've never personally had to resort to this method, but I found this sigil while researching and thought it was interesting and worth sharing.

It also goes without saying that you can create your own sigils for spirit banishment.

Faust's grimoire says to draw this sigil on a Monday during the hour of Jupiter, which for Mondays will be the 3rd hour of daylight, typically between 8 and 9 AM.

Protection Stone

Find a stone with a high vibration, to do this hold a stone in your hand and feel its energies. Take the stone outside and find a peaceful place to sit. Stare into the stone, ground yourself, and charge the rock with energy and intention. Say the following:

*"Stone, evil shall you deny.
Send it to the Earth and sky.
Send it to the flame and sea,
Stone of power, protect me."*

You can carry this stone with you, keep it in your home or give it to someone else to protect them.

Goal Accomplishment Jar Spell

This ritual is designed to keep one on a desired path, whether you're trying to quit a bad habit, studying for an exam, learning a new trade, dieting and exercise or any other number of goals you wish to accomplish.

You will need:
Dirt or sand
Pepper flakes (any kind will do)
Red candle
Bind rune of perseverance
Glass jar with lid

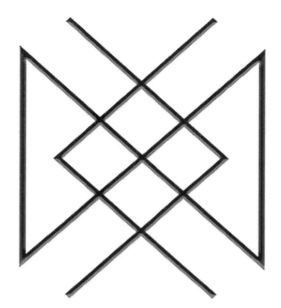

"bind rune of perseverance"

Focus on accomplishing your goal and carve the bind rune into the candle. This bind rune is a combination of the Dagaz and Othala Futhark runes. The Dagaz runes represents the daily cycles of life while Othala represents positive accumulated outcomes, generally wealth and status from the accomplishments of you and your ancestors.

Put your dirt into the jar as your base. Add a few dashes of pepper flakes into the jar. Light the red candle and meditate on your goals and how you will accomplish them. Drip some of the candle wax into the jar. You can speak your intentions to your god, goddess or spirit and ask them to aid you in achieving your goals. Give thanks to your deity and make an offering if you'd like.

Meditate on what your life will be like once you accomplish your task and see yourself transcended to this new position. Seal the jar with the wax and extinguish your candle to conclude the ritual.

Keep the jar in a safe place and don't open or dispose of it until you've achieved your goals or you no longer wish to pursue those goals.

Aphrodite Beauty Oil

Not only is this oil great for your hair and skin, but it will also gift you with the radiant blessings of Aphrodite! With this you'll want to follow the directions and not substitute any of the oils for others as some oils can damage your skin or hair if used in improper amounts. Jojoba and Almond are great bases for oil mixtures as they don't clog your pores and aren't harmful in any amounts, our additive will be lavender, which has been shown to promote hair growth and prevent thinning, it's also one of my favorite scents!

You will need:
2 Oz of jojoba or almond oil
5 drops of lavender oil
Glass bottle

Mix the oils together in the bottle and say the following:

> *"Aphrodite, bless this oil,*
> *Elevate this mortal coil.*
> *Radiant, shining, blissful beauty,*
> *Proudly displayed for the world to see!"*

Put a few drops into the palm of your hand and rub together. You can lightly apply this oil to your hair and skin to look, smell, and feel great!

To Prevent Nightmares

You will need:
3 white candles
teaspoon of spearmint leaves
Infuser (optional)
Hot water
Tea cup

Put the spearmint leaves into the glass and add the hot water.

Place the three candles in a triangle around the glass, with the glass in the center.

Say the following:

*"I am safe while I sleep, there is nothing to fear.
For now I understand, nothing can hurt me in here."*

Blow out the candles and drink the water, don't swallow any of the leaves, you can use a spearmint teabag or tea infuser to make things easier. Repeat this ritual every night for about a week, after that you can start spacing out your need to perform the ritual. Eventually you will be free of nightmares without the need of the ritual.\

Basic Healing Spell

Place your hands near the site of the pain, palms facing the source of the pain. Close your eyes and envision the pain coming out as a small thread. Slightly and slowly pull your hand back as the thread follows. As you feel the energies in your palms building cast the energies up and away with a quick motion of your hand.

While this spell is basic and doesn't require much ritual, being able to perform it typically requires years of practice and meditation on the healing arts. Advanced practitioners can use this spell to heal others as well as themselves.

Pentacle Ward Spell

You will need:
Sage smudge stick
Sandalwood incense

Start by meditating until you reach the point of complete tranquility. You need to empty your mind of all negative thoughts and feelings. Place a stick of sandalwood incense in each room of your home. Pray to your deity for the protection of your home and family.

Light your smudge stick and start by tracing a pentacle in the air in the windows and doors of each room. Start at the lower left-hand part of the pentacle and imagine a dome forming over your home. This spell needs to be redone every month because the wards lose power over time. Finish by giving thanks to your favored god/goddesses.

Cleansing/Charging a New Wand

Wands allow us to better focus our intentions while spellcasting. Wands can carry residual energies from previous owners or the maker of the wand so it's always a good idea to do a cleansing ritual and charge it anew.

You will need:
Copper cauldron (or pot)
Sea saltwater
Incense
Quartz crystal
Wand to be cleansed
Flowers, gemstones and or rose quartz.

Boil water in the copper cauldron and mix in a dash of sea salt. Stir three times and say:

*"May the goddess enter the water,
may the goddess make it pure."*

Leave the cauldron to cool in the garden (or a grassy area) in a sunny spot and say the following:

"May Apollo's rays fill you with power"

Make a circle around your cauldron with the flowers and stones. Add a crystal to the cauldron or pot. It should take about an hour to cool. Light the incense and place the wand into the now cooled water. Say the following:

"May Apollo's light be released!"

Remove the wand from the water and stir the water three times clockwise.

Allow the wand to dry on your windowsill.

Garden Growth Spell

What you will need:
Amethyst or obsidian stone
Small bowl of water
Thorns (from a rose or other plant)
feather
Leaves or flower petals

Cast a circle around your garden by placing the stone on the north end of the garden to represent Earth, the feather to the East for Air, the thorns to the South for Fire, and the bowl of water to the West.

Stand at the south end of your garden and face north, say the following:

"Earth, Air, Fire, Water, and spirit!
I call on thee to protect my garden and help it grow!
Spirit protect, Earth nourish, Water feed, Fire guard, and Air lift up!
Hear my call and come to me,
This is my will so mote it be."

Tend to your garden daily, give thanks to the elemental spirits that watch after your garden alongside you. Spend time in your garden and learn as much about it as you can, how it grows, breaths, and ebbs with cycles of the year. Respect your garden, treat it as an extension of your craft and it will reward you with a bountiful harvest.

Second Sight, Third Eye Ritual

Many ancient cultures and religions were aware of the third eye. They believed it to be related to a small eye-shaped endocrine gland in the brain called the pineal gland. The Eye of Horus is believed to be a representation of this gland, and it is also related to the root chakra in Hindu beliefs. This is a simple ritual to work on developing your third eye which will increase clairvoyance and overall magical abilities.

You will need:
Purple candle
Amethyst

I'll be using a purple candle as it represents the crown chakra and an amethyst as it is thought to stimulate the third eye.

Light your candle and/or incense and sit in a comfortable position. Hold the amethyst between your eyes and focus on your third eye opening up. Envision it inside your head getting stronger, power radiating from its core. Place the amethyst in front of you and meditate for as long as you can, I try to meditate for at least ten minutes at a time.

Do this ritual regularly and over time you will develop the ability of second sight as your third eye opens. It's possible to see a difference immediately after one ritual, but not common. Great power comes with practice and study! Your second sight is similar to a muscle in that your abilities of clairvoyance will grow with usage.

Ritual of Undoing

When a spell doesn't go as desired, whether it be a lack of focus, misdirected intention, or unexpected outcomes, it's good to perform a ritual of undoing to prevent any further harm. Think of it as sending energies out to negate the ones you wish to undo.

You will need:
Isa Rune
Paintbrush/paint or pen
Parchment/paper

"Isa Rune"

Isa is the Futhark rune of ice and represents binding, freezing cold and is the opposite of Fehu, the rune of movement. We'll be using Isa to freeze and negate those energies from the spell you wish to undo. Place your parchment in front of you and draw a large pentacle with your paint or pen, inside the pentacle draw the Isa rune. While thinking of the spell you wish to undo say the following:

"Freezing winds come blowing thru,
Chill these forces I wish to undo,
Frozen in place, impotent now,
Only released if I allow."

Sigil Magic

Sigils are symbols that are used as representations for a god, goddess, or other spiritual entity. They can also be created and charged by a practitioner to achieve a desired outcome. So, in a way, they are like spells in that we use them to accomplish our needs.

In medieval magic, sigils were used to represent various Angels and Demons and there were many magical training books for sigils, called grimoires. A well-known grimoire from this era, "The Lesser Key of Solomon", lists 72 sigils which correspond to 72 demons of hell. Sigils were considered to be a type of "true name" for these entities and gave the practitioner a measure of control over these magical beings. A common method of creating these sigils were to convert the names of the spirits into numbers and plot them on a magic square. The points would then be connected by lines to form an abstract symbol representing the entity to be used in ritual work to worship or invoke the spirit.

Witches today generally use sigils to create affirmations and to affect change in their lives by creating sigils that are charged with our intent. There are many methods to create sigils and it can really be anything that represents any sort of concept that you wish to manifest.

When doing sigil magic to manifest something, you generally start out with a statement of intent. Avoid negative statements such as "I will not be anxious" and opt for a positive statement such as "I am calm and confident". Here's a few examples of statements of intent.

"My family is healthy and strong"
"Self-confidence"
"I desire inner peace"
"I wish to honor the goddess"

For this example, we're going to use "My family is healthy and strong".
From this point, you simplify this statement as much as possible to create an abstract symbol that represents your desire.

Cross out any letters in the sentence that repeat. You may also cross out vowels (AEIOU) to further simplify the sentence. So, the letters you will be left with in this example are:

"MYFLSHTNDRG"

Now use all these letters to create a symbol that represents your desire: in this case, for your family to be healthy and strong. You can be as creative as you wish when creating your symbols. Your letters can be of differing sizes and can be flipped in any direction as you construct your sigil. There are other advanced methods to create sigils that involve plotting out the letters on a grid, usually circular, and then connecting the points to make your sigil. I'll be showing you the method which, in my opinion, is most beginner-friendly and holds just as much power as the more advanced methods.

Symbols can overlap to further simplify the sigil. For example, the following symbol can be used as a simplified version of the letters S Y V and L, each letter making up parts of other letters.

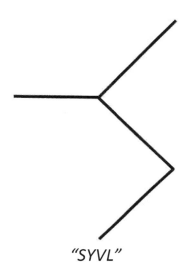

"SYVL"

You can use straight lines, curves, or abstract symbols to create your sigils. The important thing is that the symbol represents your intent.

Now, our statement of intent is, "my family is healthy and strong" and the letters we reduced it to are "MYFLSHTNDRG". Let's put them all together, see what we get and then go from there:

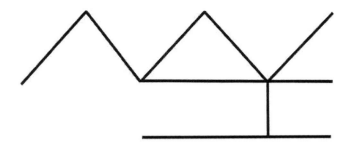

    This symbol contains all the letters compiled into a single image. Now, from this point you can further simplify the symbol or continue with the creation of your sigil. I'd like to make my symbol a bit more simplified so that when I create the circle for the sigil everything is compact and fits nicely without being too wide or narrow. As you can see, I started with the M and added all the letters on from there. I'm going to further simplify it by taking the left half of my M and moving it over to the other side, to make a more ideal abstract symbol for my sigil.

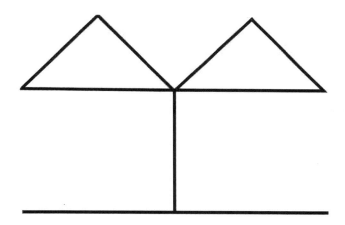

At this point you can draw a circle around your sigil or cut it out to create an area where the energies you transfer to the sigil will be contained.

Now it's time to activate your sigil. This step involves clearing your mind and focusing solely on your desires and channeling those desires into your sigil. There are a number of ways to charge the sigil: chanting, dance, song, orgasm, meditation. However, what you are essentially doing is focusing your intentions and energies and directing them into the sigil.

After your sigil has been charged and activated, you are free to do with it as you see fit. Many choose to destroy the sigil by tearing, burning, soaking, burying, or any other means of destruction. You can also do this by cutting or erasing the lines, releasing the energies of the sigil back into the cosmos.

In traditional Chaos Magick you "forget" the sigil at this point. By putting the sigil out of our minds, we allow it to work in our subconscious as a symbol representing the intention and the words we used to create it. This allows the sigil to do its work, undisturbed by our conscience minds bombardment of unintended intentions which might influence the workings of the sigil.

This is just a basic way to conduct sigil magic and there are many other methods that vary from practitioner to practitioner. You can get as creative as you like: there's no correct way to construct your sigils. The important thing is that you're creating a symbol that represents your intentions.

Look into the flame of the center candle and erase the image of the target from your mind. Take a sip of the moon water and offer the rest to the Goddess while giving thanks for her counsel and wisdom.

Divination

Divination is the process of using objects such as cards or runes to better understand our past, present, and future. We use these interpretive tools to connect us to the divine and the cosmos for understanding and guidance. Divination has been practiced by pagans, witches, and heathens for thousands of years and is one of the most ancient magics known to mankind. Like everything in witchcraft there are multiple methods to achieve the same goal so feel free to use whatever methods and tools you that you feel most connected to.

Some of the more common forms of divination use tarot cards, rune casting, spirit boards, bones, candle wax, and various forms of scrying. You might hear of water-, crystal ball-, smoke- or candle-gazing which are also forms of scrying. Any of these, or a number of other tools, can help you develop your intuition and give you insight into different aspects of your life and the lives of others with practice.

Divination takes much practice, and you will likely find that some methods work better for you than others. As you become more familiar with the practice you will strengthen your intuition, develop your spiritual-self, and become more skilled in the art of divination.

While most people might think of fortune-telling when they hear divination, the true power of divination lies in being able to see the forces that have, are, and will affect our past, present, and future so that we may adapt, grow, and change our current and future situations. Think of divination as a way of looking at the threads of fate and the forces that surround them.

For example, if you have a negative reading or sign pertaining to the future, don't get upset. The future is not set in stone and through divination we are able to see our current trajectory and course correct to achieve a better outcome. In contrast, good or positive signs let us know that we are currently on the right path to where we want to be. As you become more experienced, you will get better and better at interpreting the signs and what they mean regarding your life. Always make sure to meditate on the signs and think deeply on the information you are given and how it relates to your circumstances.

In the next section I'm going to be sharing my favorite method of divination, rune casting. Keep in mind that there are many different methods of divination, and you will likely find a way that you prefer as well as you continue down your path.

Rune Casting

Rune casting is a type of divination using runes, typically the Futhark Runes, to gain insight on our past, present, and future. The Futhark Runes are an ancient magical alphabet given to mankind by the god Odin. I'll go over the Futhark Runes and their meanings later in the book.

Rune casting is done in a similar way as Tarot. You select at random and place (cast) one, three, or more runes to get insight from the divine as it pertains to the past, present and future.

Three Norns Method

This simple beginner method is named after The Three Norns, who are Norse Goddesses and the weavers of fate. The diviner draws three runes from a bag or box and places them in front of them one at a time to reveal the past, present, future as it pertains to the situation in question. It is possible to do a general reading or ask about a specific situation.

The first rune placement is "The Place of Urd". The rune in this position reveals the past events that have a direct relation to the present situation and form the foundation of future events.

The second rune placement is "The Place of Verdandi". This rune refers to the current situation or choices that must be made in the very near future.

The third rune placement is "The Place of Skuld". This rune refers to the veiled future. This position can reveal an aspect of your future and can show where the path you are currently on will take you.

When doing any kind of divination, be preceptive to the divine. We are searching for their wisdom, and they are connecting to us and sharing their knowledge through the tools that we use during divination. Before casting, you might want to meditate on the information you wish to receive. Focus on the specific aspect of your life you're seeking guidance on. You may also wish to make an offering to your gods, goddesses, and ancestors and welcome their guidance as you look for the answers you seek.

Regardless of the method, take time after divination to meditate on the reading you receive. If you are confused, ask for clarity and be perceptive to signs you might receive. I like to keep a dream journal to record any insight I might get while dreaming because the barriers between our realm and the divine are thin in the dreamscape.

Scrying

Scrying is the practice of divining the future or seeking answers by gazing into a reflective surface such as a mirror, water, or a crystal ball.

Scrying is almost like dreaming with your eyes open. We allow ourselves to slip into a meditative state while gazing into any reflective surface. While in this receptive state, we can perceive signs that can be interpreted to get an idea of what the future may hold. Scrying takes a lot of practice and the more you learn about symbols and their meanings, the better you will become at accurately discerning what you're seeing.

When I'm scrying, I like to place a candle behind my crystal ball and gaze into the flame as it dances. I find it mesmerizing and it helps me get into a meditative state quickly, to perceive the signs my gods wish to show me. Find a way that works for you and practice, practice, practice! Scrying can be very therapeutic, will help you develop your intuition, and is a great entry level way to get into divination. While learning to scry can be easy, mastering it can take many years.

Pendulum Dowsing

Pendulum dowsing uses an object, usually a crystal that is attached to a string or chain. You then ask a question and hold the pendulum over a chart or graph. The direction the pendulum swings in reveals an answer.

The answer that the pendulum reveals isn't necessarily set in stone, because as we've learned already, fate is not set, and our course always has the potential to be changed.

Any type of chart can be used, you can even forgo the use of a chart and just designate cardinal directions as specific answers, such as north/south mean 'yes', and east/west mean 'no'.

This is just one of many ways for the divine to reveal hidden information and give guidance. Here are a few example charts that you might wish to duplicate and use for your own practice. You may also make your own!

The Futhark Runes

The Futhark Runes have been especially important to my own path. I've always felt a close connection to these ancient symbols and the gods that granted them to mankind. I meditate on the runes frequently and include them in much of my ritual work. They're also my go to form of divination.

Norse legend says that the All-Father Odin hung from Yggdrasil, The World Tree, for nine days and nights, staring into the Well of Urd. He had pierced himself with his own spear to prove he was worthy of the knowledge that the Norns possessed. On the ninth night, the Runes revealed themselves to him and granted him all the knowledge they held. Odin's powers greatly multiplied, making him one of the most powerful entities in the cosmos.

These runes can be used in divination or be directly applied to anything to imbue the magical properties that the runes represent. They can also be used alongside any ritual to boost the powers and energies of the forces represented by the runes.

FEHU (Cattle)

Germanic: Fe (Fehu)
Gothic: Faihu
Norse: Fé
Anglo-Saxon: Feo, Feoh
Icelandic: Fé
Norwegian: Fe

Fehu literally translated means 'cattle'. It is a symbol of wealth, property and prosperity. This is the rune of luck and, as such, has the capacity to harbor luck and make use of it. Fehu has the power to bless new endeavors and assist in making new goals. While being a rune of wealth, the fact that it is also directly tied to luck suggests that an altruistic nature is required to make use of its power because luck is a result of courageous deeds. Fehu is a useful rune to use when performing rituals related to wealth, luck, love and prosperity.

Stones associated with this rune are tiger eye, carnelian, citrine, and aventurine.

ÜRUZ (AUROCHS)

Anglo-Saxon: UR
Germanic: Uraz (Uruz)
Gothic: Urus
Norse: Úr
Anglo-Saxon: Ur
Icelandic: Úr
Norwegian: Ur

Aurochs were a species of wild ox that lived in the European forests until they were hunted to extinction in the 1600's. This rune represents the cosmic seed, beginnings, and origins. It is masculine in nature and gives strength, endurance and athleticism. It is a rune of courage and boldness, freedom, rebellion, and independence. Ur represents the horn or the erect phallus, resurrection, life after death, as well as coming, being and passing away.

Representing the transfer of energies, it is used for projecting or drawing in of energy. Repeated use of the rune will gradually increase the amounts of energy one can handle at any given time and helps in the growth of one's own reserves of power.

Stones associated with this rune are agate, epidote, fire agate, and diamond.

THURISAZ (Giants/Thorn)

Germanic: Thyth (Thurisaz)
Gothic: Thauris
Norse: Þurs
Anglo-Saxon: þorn
Icelandic: Þurs
Norwegian: Thurs

Thurisaz represents the Jotnar (giants) and is the rune of primal forces, destruction, conflict, and curses. Thurisaz also governs the making of tools, especially the tools of war. Use this rune to break down barriers, destroy, and transform. Chaos is the true nature of this rune, and a strong will and mind is needed to make proper use of it. This rune can be used in conjunction with other runes and spells for any number off manifestation purposes. The rune itself is constructed to visually represent a thorn, a phallic symbol, as this rune represents masculine energies and can be used in virility or impotence rituals. This rune is highly effective when used with a bloodstone and used in conjunction with hematite can be very effective in deflecting curses.

Stones associated with this rune are bloodstone, hematite, cloudy quartz, agate, and malachite.

ANSUZ (Speech)

Germanic: Aza (Ansuz)
Gothic: Ansus
Norse: Óss, Áss
Anglo-Saxon: Aesc, (Os, Ac)
Icelandic: Óss, Áss

Ansuz is a rune that refers to speech and communication. The word 'Ansuz' is thought to mean 'mouth' which is meant to infer speech. The rune represents Odin, The All-Father, and is a rune of consciousness, mysticism, and mind. It opens channels of self-expression and overcomes obstacles of every kind. It can be used in initiating oneself with Odin and assists in enhancing one's psychic and magical abilities.

Ansuz also serves as a representation of breath, which can refer to the spirit. This rune is capable of evoking inspiration and is frequently used by artists and students of the occult. It has been found on many ancient artifacts, mainly staffs and rings which are presumed to have been imbued with the power of this rune.

This rune can have many practical implications such as rituals to be more confident and outspoken. Incorporate it in a ritual to help with any issues you might be having regarding speech, whether that be stage fright or anxiety around new people.

Stones associated with this rune are lapis lazuli, moldavite, opal, and kyanite.

RAIDHO (Riding)

Germanic: Reda (Raidho)
Gothic: Raida
Norse: Reið, Reiðr
Anglo-Saxon: Rad
Icelandic: Reið
Norwegian: Reid, Reidr

Raidho refers to travel, motion, and journeys. This rune is used to reveal the best way to proceed in a given situation and can illuminate the best path to take in our lives. In German 'Rad' means 'wheel', which is where this rune derives its name, and is also where the words 'road' and 'ride' come from. In addition, the Icelandic word for advice is 'Rada' and from these meanings we can surmise what this rune represents.

The construction of this rune is a combination of the Isa and an inverted Sowilo rune. The zig-zag shape represents a journey that changes directions, moving downward along the staff of the rune. Like Ansuz, Raidho is used to represent Odin, who was known as The Wanderer and The Rider. It is a rune of travel, journeys, and physical endurance, all of which Odin was known for. It has been used as a charm for travelers and as a guide for the dead in their journey to the afterlife. You can make your own charm to carry with you by etching, drawing, or painting this rune onto a piece of wood or stone. Raidho can also be included in any rituals pertaining to travel or change.

Stones associated with this rune are opal, quartz, lolite (water sapphire), ametrine, dendritic agate and kyanite.

KENAZ (Torch)

Germanic: Chozma (Kenaz)
Gothic: Kaun
Norse: Kaun
Anglo-Saxon: Cen, Ken
Icelandic: Kaun
Norwegian: Kaun

The Kenaz rune represents our ability to harness the unseen forces of nature to illuminate our way, our ability to use the world around us to gain insight, wisdom, and security. While the Thurisaz rune represents tools, this rune represents what we're able to do with them. The torch that brightens the path before us and brings clarity to our past. This rune works great in conjunction with Ansuz when exploring ancestral connections and enlightenment. It is also the rune of feminine mysteries and knowledge and works wonderfully in any ritual involving feminine health and empowerment.

Stones associated with this rune are fire agate, fire opal, citrine, garnet, ruby sun stone and amber.

GEBO (Gift)

Germanic: Geuua (Gebo) Gothic Giba
Norse: Gipt, Giöf
Anglo-Saxon: Geofu (Gyfu)
Icelandic: Gjöf
Norwegian: Giof

Gebo is the rune of sacrifice and giving. A representation of something of personal value given freely, such as our blood when we choose to consecrate the runes in this way. This is a rune of initiation, where we make personal sacrifices to obtain knowledge, power, and wisdom such as when Odin hung from Yggdrasil for 9 days to attain knowledge.

Gebo can be utilized during any ceremony or ritual pertaining to harmony of a union, such as a contract or marriage. Gebo is also used in sex magic and as it is deeply tied to the exchange of energies between partners. Used with the Isa rune, the combination is powerful in binding enemies.

Stones associated with this rune are emerald and jade.

WUNJO (Joy)

Germanic: Uuinne (Wunjo)
Gothic: Winja
Norse: Vend
Anglo-Saxon: Wynn
Icelandic: Vin
Norwegian: Wynn

Wunjo is the rune of joy, used to bind us with those we care for and for strengthening those bonds. It is a rune of harmony, friendship, community, and family. Wunjo has the ability to banish the hurdles that foment alienation and prevent us from bonding. Use Wunjo as a ward to prevent the sorrows that would keep you from achieving your maximum level of consciousness. Community is the embodiment of this rune and all the things that make up that community: love, trust, health, and divine will.

Wunjo is commonly known as a rune of perfection and correct wishing. We can utilize the power of Wunjo to marry our dreams to our actions to achieve our maximum potential.

Stones associated with this rune are topaz and clear quartz.

HAGALAZ (Hail)

Germanic: Haal (Hagalaz) Gothic Hagl
Norse: Hagall
Anglo-Saxon: Hægl
Icelandic: Hagall
Norwegian: Hagall, Hagl

This rune represents hailstones and involuntary sacrifice with no reward. It is a rune of suffering and injustice. A rune of destruction, disaster and catastrophe. This rune is often used in black magic, sending destruction in the form of whatever runes and intentions are used with it, delivering violent loss and pain.

While this rune is typically used for harmful reasons, it can also be used to gain understanding of what we cannot control. It symbolizes fate and can be used to gain insight into our divine nature and the will of the gods. Use this rune in conjunction with other relevant runes to discover what fate has in store for you or others in trying times. For example, you can gain insight on the outcome of family ordeals by pairing this rune with Wunjo. In addition, you can attempt to alter fate by pairing this rune with Nauthiz and communing with the Norns who have power over the fates of humanity.

Stones associated with this rune are ruby, aquamarine, onyx and cassiterite.

NAUTHIZ (Necessity)

Germanic name: Noicz (Nauthiz)
Norse name: Nauð, Nauðr
Anglo-Saxon name: Nied (Nyd)
Icelandic name: Nauð
Norwegian name: Naudr, Naud

Nauthiz is the rune of endurance, will, and the mental strength needed to last. It represents the dark night of the soul and is connected to the Hagl rune. Nauthiz can be utilized to realize what we need in spite of what we desire. It has the ability to empower us with the wisdom to see what must be done in otherwise difficult situations.

When used in white magic, this rune gives defiance and the strength to carry on when all hope seems lost. It is a rune of survival and fearlessness in the face of death. When directed at another, this rune can give the spiritual strength to carry on and endure in the face of disaster.

Stones associated with this rune are obsidian, apatite, carnelian and azurite.

ISA (Ice)

Germanic: Icz (Isa)
Gothic Eis
Norse: Íss
Anglo-Saxon: Is
Icelandic: Íss
Norwegian: Is

Isa is a rune of binding. It represents stealth and is used in operations where one wishes to proceed undetected by spiritual or physical entities.

In nature, ice creeps up on the land, quietly freezing and immobilizing everything in its path while the unaware fall victim to it. Isa the rune of binding and preventing action through hidden means. It can halt a plan and prevent something from developing. It is used to conceal and can render the victim unaware of impending personal disaster to the extent that any actions attempted will be too late in coming. It is also used in preventing any action from a known hostile party. Isa freezes action and is the rune of cold, barren stillness, and death. Isa is the polar opposite of Fehu, as Fehu is a rune of movement and Isa is a rune of binding.

This rune is helpful in meditation as it acts to still the mind and help concentration, bringing calmness and guidance. Isa works to calm hysteria, hyperactivity, and restlessness. Often used in protective spells to bind an aggressor, it also helps focus the will of the operator. Used with other runes, it acts to bind and shield the energies to keep them from interacting with each other.

Stones associated with this rune are malachite, obsidian, smoky quartz, and diamond.

JERA (Year)

Germanic name: Gaar (Jera)
Gothic: Jer
Norse: Ár
Anglo-Saxon: Ger (Jara)
Icelandic: Ár
Norwegian: Jara, Ar

Jera is a rune of cycles and is symbolic of the harvest where the efforts of planting and working in the fields are rewarded with crops. Ar represents the cycles of change, including life cycles, lunar cycles, and the seasons. Jera is in contrast to Isa where everything stops. It signifies the return of the Sun and brings action. Jera symbolizes a vortex of cycling energy: the eight-fold wheel of life, the point inside of the circle, which is the glyph for the

Sun, meaning regeneration. Jera can bring a reversal of personal fortunes. Like the tarot card, the Wheel of Fortune, Jera can reverse circumstances, so misfortune is replaced with luck and visa-versa.

Jera is the rune of patience and awareness, moving in harmony with natural cycles. It is excellent for working with nature and is a rune of fruitfulness. Ingwaz is the seed planted, Berkano is the earth that receives it and Jera is the growth and the harvest. It is a rune of long-term planning and persistence that helps ensure the success of plans.

Stones associated with this rune are moss agate, lepidolite, and moonstone.

EIHWAZ (Yew Tree)

Germanic name: Ezck (Eihwaz)
Gothic: Eihwas
Norse: Elhaz
Anglo-Saxon: Yr (Ēoh)
Norwegian: Eo

The Eihwaz rune represents the yew: the tree of life and death. This rune is frequently compared to the death tarot and holds many of the same meanings. Eihwaz is a rune of transformation, death and the beginning of something new. Eihwaz can represent the reversal of a current situation, or the beginning of something new coming from the ashes of old habits or attachments. Eihwaz is designed to show the duality that is life and death and their inseparable connection. Eihwaz reminds us to not fear death. It is merely a part of the cycle of life and rebirth and should be welcomed as it heralds change and new beginnings.

Stones associated with this rune are aquamarine, gold stones, and chrysocolla.

PERTHRO (Unknown)

Germanic name: Pertra (Perthro)
Gothic: Pairthra
Norse: Perð
Anglo-Saxon: Peordh (Pertra)
Icelandic: Perð, (Plástur)
Norwegian: (Pertra)

Perthro is a rune of divination. The unknown represents our fate and the control one has over their life. Our fates are tied to our actions and luck, and with divination we can ask The Norns to give us a glimpse into what may be if we remain on our current course.

Perthro is the most mysterious of runes as it deals with the mysteries of the other runes, life itself and our relationship with them. Fate, chance, and action are undeniably linked, creating a web between ourselves, the gods, and the universe. This rune ultimately represents these links and can be used for divination purposes in conjunction with other runes or by itself to ask favor and insight from the Spinners of Fate.

Stones associated with this rune are onyx, amethyst, labradorite, and sapphire.

ALGIZ (Life)

Germanic name: Algis, Algiz or Elhaz
Gothic: Algs
Anglo-Saxon name: Eolh
Norwegian name: Elgr

Algiz is the rune of life. It is constructed in a way as to represent three branches atop the World Pillar, symbolic of a tree reaching up towards the heavens. It is a powerful rune of protection and represents the greatest defense that exists in the futhark runes, the branches represent the horns of an elk which are able to attack as well as defend.

Algiz can be used as a shield against spiritual and physical attacks. It represents the power of man and their divine fate to uphold the order created by the gods in defense of Asgard and

Midgard. It is also used in consecration and the banishing of negative energies. It is excellent for witches to wear when performing dangerous rituals as it protects against wayward disruptive energy. It can also be carved into an object and placed upon an altar or spell-space.

Stones related to this rune are amethyst, emerald, fire agate, yellow jasper, smoky quartz, kunzite, labradorite and obsidian.

SOWILO (Sun)

Germanic: Sugil (Sowilo)
Gothic: Sauil
Norse: Sól
Anglo-Saxon: Sigel
Icelandic: Sól
Norwegian: Sol Old
Danish: Sulu
Old German: Sil, Sigo, Sulhil

The rune of the Sun and the counterforce to Isa, the rune of Ice. Sowilo is a rune of action, honor, invincibility, and final triumph. It is the rune of movement that bestows the will to act. It symbolizes the chakras and the lightning bolt, the spark of life. It has both shielding and combative properties. It is used for understanding the energy forces in the world and on the astral plane. When used with other runes, it activates and empowers them. It can be used in meditation and to empower your own stores of energy. Sowilo brings out one's leadership abilities and enhances one's strength of spirit.

Stones associated with this gem are ruby, red spinel, red garnet, rubellite, and diamond.

TIWAZ (Tyr)

Germanic: Tys (Tiwaz)
Gothic: Teiws
Norse: Týr
Anglo-Saxon: Tir, Tiw
Icelandic: Týr
Norwegian: Ty

The Tiwaz rune is associated with Tyr, the sky god of justice. The rune is constructed in a way to represent a balanced spear-point which indicates movement in a single or upward direction. This rune also represents sacrifice as Tyr sacrificed his hand to bind the wolf of chaos, Fenrir.

Tiwaz is the rune of harmony, justice and the warrior. It represents honor, which is representative of the sacrifice Tyr made to uphold the cosmic order. It is used for stability and the binding of chaotic energies. It is good for defense and revenge workings as it represents justice.

Stones associated with this rune are hematite, sunstone, bloodstone, tiger eye, and heliotrope.

BERKANO (Birch Goddess)

Germanic: Bercna (Berkano)
Gothic: Bairkan
Norse: Bjarkan
Anglo-Saxon: Beroc
Icelandic: Bjarkan
Norwegian: Bjarkan

Berkano gets its name from the birch tree which represents regeneration and youth. The rune alludes to the female form and is constructed to represent the breasts and belly of a pregnant woman. Berkano represents birth and rebirth after destruction. It is commonly associated with Ostara, goddess of spring and rebirth.

This rune can be used in workings for female fertility, feminine magic, and nurturing. It is also used in concealment and protection. This rune symbolizes feminine energies and it is an old pagan custom to enclose a child at birth with the protective energies of Berkano, which remain with them throughout their lives. Berkano is also an excellent rune to utilize when farming and gardening, for example you could paint the Berkano rune on a large rock and place it in the center of your garden while asking the goddess to watch over your crop.

Stones associated with this rune are rose quartz, garnet, agate, and clear quartz.

EHWAZ (Horse)

Germanic: Eys (Ehwaz)
Gothic: Aihwa
Norse: Ehol, Ior
Anglo-Saxon: Eoh
Icelandic: Eykur
Norwegian: Eh, Eol

This rune represents the horse and is constructed in a way to appear as two horses facing one another, an allusion to the horses Árvakr and Alsviðr pulling the chariot of the Sun. It is also closely identified with Castor and Pollux, the Gemini twins. Ehwaz represents the duality of the masculine and feminine and mankind's ability to work together to achieve a common goal.

Ehwaz can be used to bless new partnerships and coalitions, whether that be marriage, friendships, group projects or the creation of alliances. When used with other runes Eihwaz unites the energies harmoniously.

Stones that are associated with this rune are agate, chrysoprase, citrine, moonstone, pear, and white sapphire.

MANNAZ (Mankind)

Germanic: Manna (Mannaz)
Gothic: Manna
Norse: Maðr
Anglo-Saxon: Mann
Icelandic: Maður
Norwegian: Madr

Mannaz represents the link between mankind and the gods, our shared ability of mind and memory that lead us to great things. Mannaz has a type of twisting in its structure, representing how the fates of mankind and the gods are intertwined and cannot be undone. The shape of the rune is two Wunjo runes facing one another, one representing man and the other the gods.

The Mannaz rune is often used in prophetic magic and can be utilized to commune with and honor the gods. It is a rune of destiny, fate, and potential and can be used attain wisdom and better understand out place in the universe amongst the grand order of things.

Stones that are associated with this rune are sapphire, celestite, agate, moonstone, and tiger's eye.

Laguz (Water)

Germanic: Laaz (Laguz)
Gothic: Lagus
Norse: Lögr
Anglo-Saxon: Lagu
Icelandic: Lögur
Norwegian: Laukr

Laguz is a rune that is meant to symbolize downward flowing water that is full of energy. It also represents the concept of quantity as opposed to quality. The downward slope in the rune represents water flowing downhill. Laguz also represents unbridled chaotic energy and the erosive forces of nature. It is a rune of becoming, a rune of progress and collective forces.

Laguz is a great rune to incorporate into any ritual that grants endurance and willpower, especially rituals that help with setting and achieving goals.

Stones associated with this rune are lapis lazuli, azurite, amethyst, aquamarine and sapphire.

INGWAZ (Seed)

Norse: Ing, Ingvarr
Gothic: Iggws
Germanic: Enguz (Ingwaz)
Anglo-Saxon: Ing
Icelandic: Ing
Norwegian: Ing

Ingwaz is the rune of isolation, used for preparing a space for new growth to begin. It is the rune of gestation and internal growth. It represents the ancient image of God, Ing, and is the rune of male fertility. Creative action, stored energy, and power from meditation are all good examples of Ing, it is a rune of action and everything needed to perform that action. The idea of sacrifice is a core component of Ingwaz: for something new to come about there must be something that is let go - an internal or external change must occur, this might manifest in the form of time lost as you learn a new skill or study for an exam or it might mean in order for you to grow you have to separate yourself from a person or group of people.

One of the main reasons a spell or ritual might fail is the failure of the practitioner to make the necessary sacrifices to achieve their goals and Ingwaz can help us understand what they might be. Use this rune as part of a pre-casting meditation ritual to better understand what is needed from you for your manifestation to be successful. Another great way to utilize this rune is for the purposes of separating your mind from distraction to focus on the task at hand.

Stones associated with this rune are zircon, peridot, prehnite, and tanzanite.

DAGAZ (Dawn)

Germanic: Daaz (Dagaz)
Gothic: Dags
Norse: Dagr
Anglo-Saxon: Daeg
Icelandic: Dagur
Norwegian: Dagr

The counterpart to the Jera rune, Dagaz represents the daily cycle in the same way that Jera represents the yearly cycle. Both are runes of change. Dagaz is the rune of spiritual awakening and is a symbol of light. The construction of the rune is that of an infinity symbol or an overturned hourglass, representing timelessness and limitless potential.

This rune is used to attain inspiration and enlightenment. Meditate with this rune to discover the answers to problems or blocks you've been facing. As its name entails, Dagaz can shine light on an otherwise ambiguous situation and can be useful in any ritual involving answers and understanding.

Stones associated with this rune are lapis lazuli, moonstone, sunstone, ruby, and jade.

OTHALA (Homeland)

Germanic: Utal (Othala)
Gothic: Othal
Norse: Oðal
Anglo-Saxon: Otael (Ethel)
Icelandic: Óðal
Norwegian: Ödal

Othala governs any matter dealing with ancestry, inheritance, family and estate. Similar to Fehu, it is a rune of wealth and property but where Fehu represents the beginnings of wealth and its transformation over time, Othala represents immovable wealth that has been generated by your ancestral line to be passed down to newer generations.

Othala can be used to celebrate the lives of our ancestors, praise their accomplishments and bless the legacies they left behind to help us carry on their names.

Stones associated with this rune are citron, green jade, tigers eye, rose quartz

WHEEL CALANDER

In Closing

I hope you enjoyed my book of spells! The world of magic is vast and there is a seemingly limitless wealth of information on countless topics so let this book be a steppingstone on your own spiritual path. If you enjoyed this book, check out my beginner witchcraft book *The Craft,* it's full of information regarding the history and current practices of modern witchcraft.

If you have a moment, please leave a review for the book on Amazon! I self-publish all my books and it really helps as I don't have a publisher advertising my content. Thank you for reading my book and blessed be!

Disclaimer: Always take safety precautions when

doing any ritual. Be careful if using stoves or any heat sources and always make sure to have proper ventilation. This information is educational and religious, it is not to be taken as professional medical advice, always consult with a medical professional first and foremost. Use this book at your own peril: I'm not responsible for any unintended consequences. Never ingest anything unless you're completely sure it's safe and you aren't allergic. Always be wary of the potential risk of forcing your will onto others as there can be unintended consequences. Do not commit any crimes, such as trespassing, when conducting your rituals: I don't have a spell to get you out of jail!

    Much love,
    Brittany

Printed in France by Amazon
Brétigny-sur-Orge, FR